D1712871

Cries from the Ark

Cries from the Ark

Dan MacIsaac

Brick Books

Library and Archives Canada Cataloguing in Publication

MacIsaac, Dan, 1959–, author
Cries from the ark / Dan MacIsaac.

Poems.
Issued in print and electronic formats.
ISBN 978-1-77131-470-1 (softcover).—ISBN 978-1-77131-472-5
(PDF).—ISBN 978-1-77131-471-8 (EPUB)

I. Title.

PS8625.A237C75 2017   c811'.6   C2017-902791-3
                                          C2017-902792-1

We acknowledge the Government of Canada, the Canada Council
for the Arts, and the Ontario Arts Council for their support of our
publishing program.

The author photo was taken by Bernadette MacIsaac.
The book is set in Scala.
The cover image is by Mashuk.
Design and layout by Marijke Friesen.
Printed and bound by Sunville Printco Inc.

Brick Books
431 Boler Road, Box 20081
London, Ontario N6K 4G6

www.brickbooks.ca

For Bernadette, Beni, Tobi, and MC, with love

CONTENTS

Proverbs from the Ark   1

The First Bestiary

Manx Metamorph   5
Chilcotin Wild Horses   6
Bison: Wallowing   8
Bison: Calving   9
Bison: Rut   11
Bull Moose   12
Spirit Bear   13
Garbage Bear   14
Black Bear: Filicide   15
Giant Pandas   16
Foxy   17
Sloth   18
Vancouver Island Wolverine   19
Tasmanian Tiger   20

That Bloody Pool of Trouble

Cain   25
Drunk   26
David   27
The Ear of Malchus   28
The Fisherman of Malta   30
Paul on the Adriatic   32

Raucous on the Wing

Archaeopteryx   35
Goldfinch   36
Northern Shrike   37
Redtail   38
Red Dorking   39
Red Pileated Woodpecker   41
Temptation   42
Layer   43
Great Auk   44
Crows   45
Snowy Owl   46
Owl Pellet   47
Turkey Vulture   48
Turkey Vultures   49
Chernobyl   51

Printmakers

Footprints at Laetoli, Tanzania   55
La Brea Woman   56
Cave Paintings   58
Franz Marc's *Wild Pigs (Boar and Sow)*, 1913   60
Ship in a Bottle   62
Omens of Cortés   64
Thunderbird   65
Charlotte Small   66
Maasai   68

A Brambled Kingdom

Foundations of Cages   71
Spring   73
Hail   74
Glacier Lily   75

Dandelions   76
Pommes de Terre   77
Indian Pipe   78
The Horsefly   80
Wasps   82
Surrogate   83
Woolly Bear Caterpillar   85
Tent Caterpillars   86
Termite Queen   87

Deluge

Swimming in Stone   91
La Brea Woman Redux   92
Seahorse   94
Columbus and Isabella   95
Torrington   98
Moorish Idol   99
Glass Sponges   101
Sea Star and Mussel   102
Jellyfish   103
Deluge   104

Notes   107
Acknowledgements   108

Proverbs from the Ark

Never send a raven
to do a dove's work.

Fear fills an ark;
faith empties it.

Steer toward rocks.

Animals eat their betters.

A tiger's hunger is gentler
than a youth's boredom.

The wayward son must drown.

Salt in the blood;
blood in the water.

Send a single raven
but a flock of doves.

A raven is the brother of Cain;
Eve the sister of doves.

Abel kept doves;
Cain netted them.

Like Leviathan's back
in a rising tide is the Lord.

Like a dove's wing
over still water is the Lord.

A rainbow cannot be grasped.

Commandments in stone;
vows in light.

Always reach is the rainbow's vow.

The raven is ever returning.

Never send a dove
to do a raven's work.

The First Bestiary

Manx Metamorph

Slick with spray, a laggard cat slinked
late for the evac. Lush tail caught
in the cypress door and guillotined,
waste in the wash, castaway in flood.

At the dove's arc and tide's black turning,
that fifth limb drifted to sludge. Quivering,
it took root—covenant of cattails
ringing a brash new world of wetlands.

Chilcotin Wild Horses

They died off
during the last ice age,
and for a century
of centuries
only the wild grass
remembered.

Broomtails blunt-toothed
and rough-hoofed,
a cayuse herd
stole back, crossbred
from buffalo runners
and a claim-jumper's plug.

Flesh foaled
from lean Andalusians
shipwrecked in America,
drawn north
across sierra spine
and salt lakes.

Now from pine scrub
to parched grassland,
the free herd thunders,
hides scarred
by snag and thorn,
not spurs.

Hoofbeats rattle
in a volcano's
dead throat,
crackle across
black rocks
to open plain.

Scoured again
by colossal ice
or scorched by
seismic fire,
the Chilcotin
turns barren.

Wild planets
wheel, gyre,
stampede—
first horses
again on that prairie
of hurtling starlight.

Bison: Wallowing

Hewn from humus,
chalk, and clay,
the bull bison
bows down, seething
like a hot spring.

Weighed down
by a boulder skull,
this wall of sod
flops into a wallow
of churned manure.

Under an iron flail of flies,
it contorts and writhes,
sweating out ticks
from its soiled hide
into the suety ooze.

Bison: Calving

Tipped out,
this split sack
of jumbled bits
lands on hardpan,
junkyard
of taiga.

From that burst
trash bag,
a soused thing
stilts up,
all twisted strings
and mismatched parts.

This wet puppet
lists and staggers
across grit
and flint,

throat dry
as rock salt,
drawn by thirst
cut deep
as a gulch.

Under the barbed
lash of flies,
the bull calf reels
and totters back
to its stamping,
snorting, strung-out
dam

where in the shadow
of that heaving belly
the black udder
leaks.

Bison: Rut

In the orbit
of instinct,
lust hones.

Beasts stare,
stamp, glare,
stomp.

Horns hook;
breath frosts
the air.

Slow fusion
switches
to rage.

Accelerants rush;
fire-skulls
propel.

Electrons
and protons
crash, black

holes collapse
as titans
burn down

to iron.

Bull Moose

This granddaddy is
hunchbacked, sail-eared,
flagrantly snouted,
bearded below the lip
like Honest Abe,
antlers splayed
like South Sea palms,
back end too big
for his britches,
a warehouse gut
stuffed with pin cherry,
water lily, and cress,
hairy-legged as
half of a tarantula
but stilted like a pair
of red-crowned cranes
in the Dynasty
of Song.

Spirit Bear

Ursus americanus kermodei

At the river's black mouth,
the white bear waits
for the swimmer.

He crashes into shallows,
seizing the quick fish,

glisten of silver
along cinder lips.

A cedar twig
cracks.

He lunges
for the far shore
murky with hemlock.

He vanishes—
froth spattered
on dark rock.

Garbage Bear

Quarter-ton vermin
toppling steel bins,
brash and ruinously loud
as a steel band,

bursting into a bruin buffet
of stale-dated Spam,
spattered antifreeze,
and gouts of chain oil.

Putrid smorgasbord,
spoils not fit for a goat,
bolted down. It knows
want, close cousin
to the foul horn of plenty.

Black Bear: Filicide

Winter blackout
broken by hunger,
the boar, dark Cronus,
plunges through drift
after the reek of carrion,
odour of entrails,
retched stench,
even the scent
of cubs born blind.

Giant Pandas

Contrary creatures,
carnivores evolved to live on shoots,
bear-cats that the Ming Chinese
believed ate copper cooking pots.
Bulky as beer kegs,
they must slip each hemp-line snare
then dodge each hunter's blind,
becoming addled blurs
to the poacher's eye.

Jailbirds, black-patched
lifers hostage
to the flowering
of bamboo,
under house arrest
they pace, tagged
and monitored,
kept to high ground
by slash and burn.

Tinged snowdrift
and deep tree-shade,
they just blend in,
knowing their place.
Shy cousins
to burly cave bears,
they slink through time,
discrete and buttoned-down
as butlers.

Foxy

Vulpes vulpes

You scavenge so lightly on the fringe,
flitting from hummock to highbush cranberry,
flushing varying hares and taiga voles
under the cardinal's beady eye.
Minding the high price on your red coiffure,
you dance just outside the range of buckshot.
Knowing your poison—strychnine—by scent,
you skirt each well-placed and well-seasoned bait.
The best-laid leghold traps do not tempt,
so practiced are you at saving your own hide.
Where are your pranks, your dodges and deceptions?
Hunting at the world's scalloped edge, you shift—
and vanish. Illusion is just business.

Sloth

Icon of verdigris
and pale lichen,

odalisque
pelted with algae,

ark of beetles
and moon moths,

paralytic rooster
mute as a burl.

Slow lover
of red hibiscus

and tossed,
fragrant leaves,

hanging sabre-
clawed

and masked
like a robber.

Torpid idol
suited

for drowsy
sin.

Vancouver Island Wolverine

Gulo gulo vancouverensis

Skunk-bear stinking
of dead meat,
no cuddly poster child
for the imperilled Wild.

Unseen for
half a century,
down to one straggler
dodging deadfall.

None captive-bred
then loosed
to wreak havoc
on trappers.

Embedded in crag,
denned in talus,
it became its own
cache of carrion

and never was missed—
the less said
of monsters
the better.

Tasmanian Tiger

Shot dead in 1930,
the last wild one
skulked too close
to Batty's henhouse.

Slayer breed,
long extinct,
its haunt gone
viral.

The last live one snarls
in a gritty black-and-white clip,
ghost skulking in limbo,
caught in wireless internet.

Grey tiger gapes,
iron maw
lethal as a leg-
hold trap.

Dare we hot-wire
horror, forge
terror from mere
scraps of DNA—

bare shreds bred
from filched tissue,
poached hide,
and spoiled marrow?

What were-thing
will be scorched
into being, ignited
by the brain's hot coils?

That Bloody Pool
of Trouble

Cain

Again my brother's tattered flock
of half-wild goats and horned ewes
strayed into my greening fields.
All greed and want, they
trampled the sprouting seed
and tore at the fresh millet shoots.
Again they dropped stickle burrs
and thistledown from the wasteland
into my furrows. Curse him—
a man more sloth than shepherd.
He left me only last year's grain,
grey with mold, for my offering.
For sacrifice, Abel lugged a kid
by the hooves toward the altar.
It was a starved beast near dead
from mites and its belly bloated
with black water. Roughly,
he slit the beast's throat
and dumped the flesh on broken sticks
heaped on the high rock,
the rank spoilage soon disguised
by charring flames. My rage
pried from the earth a jagged stone;
and I broke Abel open like a spring field.
I harrowed my young brother,
and threshed him like harvest grain.
I wanted to scatter his spirit
like chaff, but the voice of his blood
sang out from the soft, wet ground.

Drunk

Gut heaving,
forty nights of spume.

Skull bashed—
hooves in a barred stall.

Brain tolled—
pitch of ark.

Eyes pierced—
night crow's baubles.

Heart slamming
ribs to wreckage.

Lungs fetid,
vile as bilge.

Gullet scorched—
hell's salt bile.

Tongue writhing,
serpent's spine

splintering under
a slaver's lash.

Prophet's word
ruptured into curse.

David

...and the woman was very beautiful to look upon.
—2 Samuel 11:2

I throw myself into the perfumed sea
of Saul's harem but cannot drown you.
Those waves cast me onto cold sand;
cresting breasts collapse into sackcloth,
and fresh spume ebbs to an oily slick.
Remembering, my mouth is a ring of ash.
Sucking down brackish water, I retch dry.
So I drink a camel's load, a vat
of Gibeon wine, and still cannot forget
the sight of you moonlit in the garden,
burning white stone at my eyes and brain
uncooled by any living water.
I thirst. There is only your beauty.

The Ear of Malchus

Then Simon Peter having a sword drew it,
and smote the high priest's servant,
and cut off his right ear.
                              —John 18:10

The brats of Caiaphas the high priest
would plead to hear again how that hothead
hacked off my ear. And I would be coaxed
into telling the tale—up to the blow
by the madman's apostle. Leaving them
stranded in that bloody pool of trouble,
I'd stall, mute, until the children shrieked
again and again. Heavily, I'd sigh.
Picking my way along the story's path,
I'd describe my mangled ear in the grass—
a pulpy, torn fig—and how, with a gnarled hand,
the Nazarene touched the stump on my skull.
Swearing my small listeners to secrecy,
I'd confide how pain pulsed as a new ear
bloomed from my head like a pale mushroom.
What did you hear? the brats would always ask.
Everything, I would insist, *Everything.*
As if a god had touched me, I'd understood
the praise of birds, the buck goat's bleating,
foxes bickering in the lion's shadow,
the keen, scalloped blades of the east wind,
dark women murmuring at the village well,
and the strange music of distant stars.
Tell us, the children would beg, *tell us more.*
What do the beasts say—and the stars mean?
But I would shake my head, remembering
their father's storms, his terrible rage

flaring like fire through dry thorn bush,
and, worse, his discreet denunciations—
a pit viper coiled and hissing in its hole.
The high priest was quick to find heresy.
And I'd shiver, remembering his part
in the killing on that cold dark hill.

The Fisherman of Malta

And when Paul had gathered a bundle of sticks,
and laid them on the fire, there came a viper
out of the heat and fastened on his hand.
                    —Acts 28:3

Breakers stranded the survivor,
a bundle of sodden rags
flung ashore on a rough plank.
We turned away, kept busy
by the allure of the better-dressed,
stripping trinkets and trimmings
from corpses humped on the stones.
The yield was poor,
all cargo being sunk at sea.
The castaway stared past surf,
eyes bright as the greaves
torn from the shins
of a cold centurion.

After we had snatched
the last baubles from the dead,
the live one followed us upland.
He made himself useful,
scurrying around for dry sticks.
His bundle dropped on our fire,
a rock viper writhed out
like a barbed whip
and clamped on his right hand,
above the burled knuckles,
below the rope-burned wrist.
The adder's bite judged him

30

a cutthroat. We saw
he owed the old blood price,
eye for eye, tooth for tooth.

We waited for death:
the hand to bloat
black as a leech,
his spine to wrench
under the lash of poison,
his mouth to gnarl
and froth like a rabid dog's.
But he shook off the snake,
a hank of hair into the fire.
It sizzled, hissed, reeked.
Without a word, he turned
back to the shore.
On his hand—no fang mark,
no scalding kiss.

So we followed him,
knowing he took on
the power of the adder.
Venom did not maim.
I sailed with him east
across the sea to Rome
where I watched him
granted Nero's mercy,
beheaded cleanly by blade—
gladius—a citizen's due,
not pierced by the teeth of nails,
not crushed by the slow poison
of the toppled cross.

Paul on the Adriatic

For there stood by me this night the angel of God . . .
—Acts 27:23

I have no fear of storms since I heard His voice—
my Accuser crying out of the sun.
While I am chained in the shivering hold,
the others cower and bleat to Ba'al.
But no fury can last. Light finds a way—
it streams through cracks in the throttled planks,
and illuminates the silk rigging
of a small brown spider which, huddled,
waits patiently for the first frail fly.

Raucous on the Wing

Archaeopteryx

Jura-Museum, Eichstätt

Stratum flaunts the memory of bone,
exposing an aura of ancient plumes
hammered true out of quarried stone.
At the scorched edge of a foul lagoon,
fire, sour air, and raw earth fused.
Where in time roosts the primeval bird?
Imagine, unshackled, this flint-locked thing:
a warped brute lurching to a ragged pine,
laboriously, bristling with clawed wings,
hauling its bulk up the red bark, scrabbling
for wind that bears the shrill reek of carrion.
Through spiked teeth a forked tongue slithers,
flickers, tasting black blood in the air.
These jaws were not shaped to sing.

Goldfinch

Gypsy-bird,
glutton of thistle seed,
flits down
and out.

At the brink,
it slips in and out
of harm's way—
a rumour, almost.

Its augury
seems accidental,
plummeting to
the mockery of thorns.

No golden raptor,
it veers and yaws,
plumes not gilt
but yellow.

Its nest, lined
with thistledown,
coddles
blemished pearls.

Its song is silvery,
semi-precious,
scored for flute,
not horn.

Northern Shrike

Lanius excubitor

Grey impaler
fills its larder
with voles and locusts
deep in the thorn bush;
and along the barbed
twist of the meadow fence
gapes the rictus
of a whitethroat.

Two-ounce killer,
elfin butcher
with tiny cleaver
and lethal hook
pierces clumsily
on littered ground
or kills cleanly
in mid-air.

Deadly mimic,
voice rings
both false and true
across the ragged hedgerow
and abandoned field,
capturing each
pure pewter note
of its duped prey.

Redtail

Fiery-tailed troll
inscribes omens
with wingstrokes,

libellous pinions,
feathers multitudinous
and scarlet-lettered.

Fleet deceiver,
stooping to conquer,
crashes shy prey

that bolts
from thorn hedge
or black hole.

Under the viral
surge of sun,
brio of passage,

death uploading
its dark vigor
into the flaring bird.

Red Dorking

Caesar's fowl transported
to the dank isle
by galley slave
for augury and fare.

Ancient strain shunned
the cast seed, foretelling
the failed campaigns,
a tyrant turning capon.

Loosed among Britons,
it bred 'til cockerels
from every hovel
skirled at dawn.

Fattened and plumped
for the Tudor's table,
it added more
and more heft

to the King's great girth,
flesh torn from breast,
Pope's nose gnawed,
and drumstick gnashed.

Now the old breed
scarcely broods,
each plucky survivor,
like Caesar's ambition

or the Monarch's pair
of ill-omened consorts,
fated for the blade.

Red Pileated Woodpecker

Headbanger,
mohawked,

with a buzz-saw
guffaw,

flaps over
the mosh pit

to batter
deadwood.

Punk bird
bashing its drum kit,

blind rage
aimed at grubs

burrowing away
from mayhem.

Temptation

A grouse
arrives lost
on the forest
path,

dragging
a dead wing
like a leaden
banner.

In performing
the exacting
yielding
ceremony

of enticingly
maimed
motion,
only

her strained,
pent-
up intensity
betrays

her attempt,
and dismays
seduction.

Layer

Mutant freakbird,
hormone-pumped,
crammed with debeaked
broilers into a battery cage
24/7 above a conveyer belt
running eggs left and shit right.

All our sci-fi fantasies
of star voyages,
extraterrestrial traffic,
and galactic superpowers
are reduced to you,

gene-spliced producer
of engineered food—
ovoid fodder fried
in greasy spoon diners,
scrambled, easy-over,
or sunny-side up.

Great Auk

Outlasted Neanderthal,
Dorset, and Beothuk,
endured Basque greed,
bounty hunters
for bait or down,
only to be doomed
by its own oddity—

each roc egg,
rare and high-fired
as a Ming jar,
turned must-have,
the old breed damned
by a bidding rigged
for the last blown clutch.

Crows

looming on a wire—
dark matter
                    dark energy—
raucous on the wing

Snowy Owl

Null bird
in the eye
of an ice storm.

Blank cipher
blown from
the northern void.

White hole
of wind
and half-light.

At zero hour,
annihilating
silence.

A
sheer
dearth.

An
absence.

Owl Pellet

Concentrate of kills—
bitter pill
of vole bones,
shrew skin,
worm bristles,
mortal coil of rat,

lark's flint beak,
finch's wing,
and rattle claws
of wren—
all encased,
embalmed.

In this retched
ossuary,
nothing remains
of any song
save feather tufts
and fluted bone.

Turkey Vulture

Scalded head
over tattered

black silk,
it mocks

the open
court of air,

ratcheting
down

to the reek
of condemned meat.

Unsightly
as the corpse,

an epicure
at death's feast,

it feeds,
sickle-beaked,

entering
at the eye,

then creaks west
to roost

on a gallows
tree.

Turkey Vultures

Dark lovebirds
blush over
a foul repast,

these corpse-
crossed lovers
eyeing flesh.

They begin
with the soft parts,
acrid hors d'oeuvres,

rancid tidbits,
delicacies of
anus and eyelid.

When the main course,
flambéed by gas,
gapes, they gorge.

Fetid spoils,
they relish,
ravish,

sour fare
shredded
to tartare.

Sated, they
stagger, wings
wine-drenched.

Connoisseurs
of fine tissues
on no casual

dinner date,
death's gourmets
mate for life.

Chernobyl

In the death zone,
black mold glowers
from concrete walls.

Midnight cancer,
radiotrophic
growth. Yet

look up,
farther, higher,
into the blue

where chiffchaffs,
blackcaps, and
barn swallows swirl—

host of archangels
circling the dark
Golgotha stacks.

Printmakers

Footprints at Laetoli, Tanzania

Four million years ago,
our ancestor walked through ash,
leaving prints passed
down to us in stone.

The trail broke
where the traveller paused
and shifted left. Distracted,
we stop and share her doubt.

La Brea Woman

Scientists speculate
she was sacrificed
nine thousand years ago,
made oblation to Earth.

Inner ear seething,
perhaps her ashen tribe
agreed only Earth
should suck that venom.

We do not know
how she died—
acceptant or frantic,
alone or with audience,
arranged or accidentally—
and thus she is more human,
broader in her suggestions.

Observe our earliest Eurydice
with whom the archaeologist,
playing Orpheus,
must fail.

The scientist may say,
I assembled her, made her.
But no, she is us,
preceding and succeeding,
our sign of bifurcation
into death and eternity.

All time her arena,
we gaze upon
an ossuary
of burnished skull
and heraldic bones.

For ninety centuries
she burned,
interred in asphalt
with a stray—
hellhound familiar,
infernal guide,
and fast friend.

The girl was gouged
out, black hole
in her tarred head,
only human
among behemoths—
monstrous sloths,
dire wolves,
and dark, shattered condors.

Unearthed, unobscured,
she stands spotlit,
forcing Earth into us.

Cave Paintings

Emblems in blood
and ash accost,

totems stroked
on dank rock.

Across stone galleries,
the first bestiary:

raw bison plunge,
avalanche of thew,

gnarled swine rush,
landslide of feldspar,

red deer rollick,
vaulting flames,

cresting surf of horses,
unbroken surge,

and the mammoth
a vast crag

as great cats
slink and skulk

to brawling
nightmare—

bullwhip hook
of claws on flank,

and ferric scrape
of fang on skull.

From limestone
wafts tang of

musk and sweat,
blood and dung.

Heartbeats,
hoofbeats,

clout of bone
on bone.

Coarse breath,
thick bristles,

scratch of barb
and talon.

Flashes of
cracked tusks,

stippled pelt,
splintered horn.

Blurry gore
of pigment,

glimmer of
flint-sparked

fire.

Franz Marc's *Wild Pigs (Boar and Sow),*
1913

Blue boar—
lunging tusks,
surly red eye—

roots and grubs
through absinthe
tint of foliage

and sulphur
caul of bloom,
unsated

as the whirlpool
of undergrowth
churns and spins.

Behind him roils
in blurred ochre
the Ur-pig.

Below him
brims and flows
the sow.

Lured here
to wallow
in oil,

these beasts
thud and roil
in muck,

possessed by
the hot stink
of paint.

Ship in a Bottle

She hails,
siren in glass,
cold virgin.

No wind arouses
those scalloped sails.
No brine corrodes
those silken lines.

The swells' caress
of slender hull
is fantasy.

Not strain of salt,
not seaweed mesh,
not knoll of barnacles
mar her form.

She calls
but no storm compels;
no anchor holds.

No sun blisters
her glossy deck.
No wave heaves
and breaks her.

Neither mastered
nor mastering,
she cannot drift.

No crew boarded her
nor scaled her masts.
No captain guides
her south.

She, queen of seas,
an argosy sealed
in a cork-stopped tomb.

No yarn to tell.
No shanty sung.
No itch of jig
in dead air.

Steered by extinct stars,
she navigates
a vacuum.

Not afloat,
not aground,
no time to clock,
no tide to run.

Mute.
Deaf.
Insensate.

Safe in
a glass womb,
unable to bear
or incubate.

Stillbirth.
Still death.
Still life.

Omens of Cortés

In the Aztec year of Twelve House:
a sign like a flaming ear of maize
blazed against heaven;

two temples torched by stealth
spat pillars of smoke;

a fire-lizard, roaring and rattling,
scattered blood-red sparks;

the lake boiled into huts,
scalding clay into hot mud;

a hag wailed like dry wind
for the doomed children;

a snared crane's glassy crest
showed the image of brute riders;

and thistle-men, two-headed stalkers,
loomed then vanished like
the steam of Popocatépetl.

Thunderbird

Cracked
by the carver's awl,

hatched
at the crag

of the steep
clan pole,

mythic as auk
or great roc,

talons cleaved
and bolted,

beak crammed
and hooked,

wings winched
and crucified,

eyes dry
lightning,

stare pitiless
as storm.

Charlotte Small

She, a Black Irish Cree,
felt the heat
of his one good eye
while she dried strips of meat.

When he spoke to her
alone in Île-à-la-Crosse,
her answers were slow
and her eyes scornful.

But her father took
the adventurer's offer,
closing a tight fist
on flint rifle and shot.

Then he yanked her
across beaver swamp
and sweetgrass prairie,
through dog-hair forest

and blue icefields,
over red mountains,
and down green rivers
to the distant sea.

She tasted salt blood
on his asylum skin
and suffered the load
of his foundling bones.

She was firmament
to his stars
and filled his orphaned mind
with heirs.

When he died,
he rattled out her name.
Her own last words
were Cree.

Maasai

Broth of milk and blood
at sunrise fuels the Maasai.
Excised vein and yanked
udder spurt, spill.

From a deep cirque of thorns,
the tribesmen goad the herd
onto lanced plains.

Prodded, cattle stagger
across parched wilderness
to the far oasis of grass.

This trek extends itself
daily, with the desert
hammered by hoofs
toward infinity.

As shadow smothers light,
at last they return,
eluding the contrary fire.

A Brambled Kingdom

Foundations of Cages

See the sleeping beauty of vines,
a brambled kingdom,
barbed braids ascending
light's trellis, up from
old foundations of cages.

As a child, I would scurry
from pen to pen to inspect
the rites of courtesan toucans,
an iguana's robotic yawn,
to-and-fro candy-cane
tails of coatimundis,

the addled whirling, swinging,
spinning of spider monkeys,
a gleam in the marmoset's
eyes, the shimmer off
a condor's scalded pate,
a barred owl's glower,

then stop to peek at hidden things
and breathe their pungencies—
thick musk of civet,
coon, and ocelot—
but never thought to set
those creatures free.

                    And I
cannot release them now.
I drift on a dark Sargasso

Sea of blackberries, afloat
over foundations eroded
by runoff, roots, and
the secret channels of vermin.

Spring

Under our porch
a child's way opens:

Chameleon fiddleheads,
lizard-shades of ferns
licking toward light.

Colonies of sowbugs,
moon-men clambering over
asteroids of wet wood.

Fungus frills
ringed and vaporous
as pale saturns.

Glutinous slugs,
amoeban mutants
expelled from ark.

A leaf shrivelled
and shredded
like cast-off snakeskin,

now a webbed
constellation patrolled
by a wolf spider.

The dank and dark
strain. This is enough.

Beneath us insists
a damp, angelic spring.

Hail

Long volleys
of frigid fire.

Spent shells
have pearls;

these are ice—
plutonic.

Despite the friction
of falling,

each layer imprisons
another Eden.

Each seed
an unbroken
maidenhead.

Glacier Lily

At the trailing
hem of snow,
suddenly Spring—
fragrant gold,
florid nugget
panned from icemelt,
perfumed bell
peals, gleaming,
glacier candled
and honeyed
with scented yield.
At the ringing margin
of pollen and crystal,
petals mingle,
coldly molten.

Dandelions

My child, on safari
through the backyard grass, picks
a pride of them as trophies.

I know in time
their manes will silver,
and my child, grown older,

will blow parachutes
of spun seed
over alien country.

Rosette cluster thrust
toward me, love seems most
like the lion's tooth.

Pommes de Terre

Ripe apples topple early,
the best bruising
against crisp earth.
Bruit of wasps.
Swallows dip.
Sun and shadows swirl
about the fallen fruit.

Sweet cider brews
inside skin.
In the aging of apples,
windfall will meld,
becoming the fork
and spring of grass.

Taste me. Touch me.
Like Eve, I smell
the ferment of the fruit.

Indian Pipe

Monotropa uniflora

Parasite beneath
spruce gloom,
sown like
dragon's teeth,

raising that brood
of pallid heads
like a hydra's ghost
from boreal humus.

From a corpse of peat,
old worm castings,
rotted needles,
and mouldered leaves

protrudes
each stem,
splintered bone
of tibia or spine.

Each bloom arcs
and lifts,
delicate
as death's rattle,

the ache
of cholera
shuddering
and pale.

Touched, it
blackens to soot;
plucked,
never revives.

The Horsefly

Old Beelzebub,
lord of flies,
you scout flesh
with bedlam eyes.

Bristly bugger,
coarse voyeur,
you skulk and cruise
secret pleasure.

Whiskery ruffian,
circling and stalking,
your siren blares
a sudden mugging.

Knives in your jaws,
grappling you board.
Bearded and hooked,
you plunder the hoard.

Demon droning
out and in,
unrelenting,
blitz again.

Immortal pest—
what if I
batter your flesh,
might you die?

Dark deceiver,
lured, I swing,
making wrath
a fruitless sin.

Old Beelzebub,
father of lies,
you mock death
with bedlam eyes.

Wasps

To that paper castle
they charge,
bristling with news
of everyday carrion
and ordinary ruin.

On furious wings
they rush the ramparts
and moat of air,
hissing slander and
scandal of decay.

Accident or chaos
draws them out,
these yellow journalists
swarming with barbed print.

Surrogate

The wasp whirls,
spry shadow cast
across a salt floor.

A tarantula lurches
like a tank;
its turret body reels.

Descending,
swift *Pepsis*
grapples to tip

the whole hulk,
plunging
her warhead in.

The crawler,
petrified,
cannot resist

as the hornet
tucks a moist egg
into that nest.

Soon the egg
shivers, cracks,
its slick worm

oozing from a slit
to suckle at
its foster dam.

Nursed by
cold blood,
it bloats

as the host
broods its own
disembowelling.

Woolly Bear Caterpillar

An idler dawdles along the late-fall path.
A dull glutton, he confronts the coming of hunger
and cold through girth and bristles, his shelter of pelt.
His barometer coat, shaggy as a Cossack hat:
the darker the bands, the harder the winter.
He will dig in against ice, against siege,
to emerge stiff and creaky as a rusted hinge
and starved in the famine of first spring, its brittle air,
before dwindling to the leanness of moth,
before floating on the thin dream of wings.

Tent Caterpillars

They pitch silver tents
in the crotch of a tree;
this harem's orgy—
a frenzy in leaves.

When the tree is stripped
and the gardener roused,
they shall eat death
in a silken shroud.

Termite Queen

This bleached queen,
tiny *Grossmutter*,
stowed away
in scrap wood.

The white madonna
glutted on cubits
of cypress, obscenely
pregnant, leaks eggs,

her descendants
gorging on
the stranded ark,
down to the dark
pitch and pegs.

Deluge

Swimming in Stone

The primeval passage
of fish was pressed
on the ancient frieze.
Supple swimmers

thrust through
time's dark annals,
the image is movement
chipped into light.

Now eye can bruise
against storied slate,
and hand can trace
the fossil's fluency.

Our senses read
the Braille of rock,
then blur—
swimming in stone.

La Brea Woman Redux

An eon ago,
she was preserved.
She took to the tar pit,
purged from her ochred tribe,
incensed by infection
smoldering in her skull.

For an era, she lay
with lions and mammoths,
the sole human smothered in tar,
pitched among terrible beasts.

Now of all her kind
which stalked the bleak plains
and skulked along the blistered shore
only she endures,
doused in amniotic oil.

Into prehistory
she sank, drowned
by a sour flood.
Acid kindled skin,
ate flesh, and riddled bone.

Grave robbers pried
her loose and set
her skeleton with steel.
Propped up in a floodlit box,
an airless coffin,
she gasps and grins—
ancient regent
and grisly figurine.

Resurrected, she deceives—
this bone helmet
stuffed with light,
this bare urn of ribs
where no heart beats.

Seahorse

Little changeling
staked to your patch
of eelgrass, your
camo shifts with mood.

You are fair game
for the dragnet,
however your hue
may flux.

Caught, you are
ground up—
quack cure
for impotence.

If only you could
transmogrify into
myth—the great
sea-steed of Poseidon,

towering and relentless
as a tidal wave
howling down
on the human shore.

Columbus and Isabella

Gold lust flared
across a gulf of blood.
The gaunt seafarer,
his thick shock of hair
bleached like sailcloth,
his sinews tight as rigging,

leaned near the pale queen,
breaching courtesy.
He smelled of salt and dust,
rough road and sea;
his words gave her vertigo,
his tongue wild as surf.

She pledged her jewels,
bloodstones once hawked
to slaughter Moors,
then collateral baubles
to blow a fool west
off the world's edge.

She made him Admiral
of all his imagined lands,
and master mariner
of three squat ships
tattooed with scarlet crosses,
a trio of square-sailed caravels

blessed against the Evil Eye,
piracies, and Saracens
to skim through weed,
fog, and breakers
to anchor at the spice coast
of the pompous East.

Plotting by dead reckoning,
he endured a mutinous crew
through the long Atlantic dark
and endless, glazed days
to claim the gold of Ophir
and pearls of Tarshish.

But in his wayward Indies,
he took in trade for glass beads,
hawkbells, and brass plate—
too little gold and plunder of souls
swindled or swapped
under the sign of his cross.

The conqueror returned
to play the part of a soft court fop,
leading a bizarre train.
Six bronze tribesmen,
salt-lashed survivors,
shouldered his haul:

an iguana hide
rough and mottled
as an ancient targe
and iron cages
of outraged,
incandescent parrots.

Light booty for a queen—
the old sea dog was kennelled
to scratch and bark.
She took stock
of this bold new world,
seeing in the glint

of Taíno nose rings
cause enough to press
from the twin kingdoms
a new crusade by wind,
to gust greed again
into the western void.

Torrington

The head stoker
was the first man downed,
lugged from the *Terror*
like a sack of steam coal.

Hunchbacked into a small hole,
shrouded in filthy cloth,
he was cached
under frozen ground.

Lead from boiler water
or tins soldered
by the lowest bidder
had clogged his blood.

His flesh, meagre
as melted wax,
floated pale as floes.

Torque of iceworms
wrenched, burst
his black lungs.

Head haloed
with frost,
jaw slung shut,

his eyes glared
against the profanity
of light.

Moorish Idol

Zanclus cornutus

Dark hijab,
bangles flashing
over old coral

clouded
with pungent
milt and ink.

Djinn lamp,
flickering,
ignites eelgrass

and sea-whips
into a bonfire
of vanities.

Torch dancer
scorches
crown-of-thorns,

spiral galaxy
of sea stars
fallen to reef.

Shadow poppet
conjured
over crushed shells

against deluge
of sea-light,
radiant tide.

Dark hijab,
bangles gleaming
over coral bleached

bare and pale
as the unblemished
page.

Glass Sponges

Ninety centuries old,
these glassy shoals
of chalices and holy grails
host swarms of sea stars,
snapper, and moon snails.

Ninety fathoms down,
though moored to marl
far under the squalls
of the hag churning
her iron cauldron,

they cannot dodge
the rock-hopper gear
of colossal trawlers
set loose like rogue bulls
dragging clamp, chain, and cable.

Sea Star and Mussel

At the tide's roiling,
a sea star clambers over armoured lines,
tapping, testing stiff crinolines.
Pentagon, bristling with crowbars,
picks a black vice, and pries, seeking
sweet, delicate parts
shielded by hardened shards.
Against the bright intruder's art,
the mussel cannot resist—shells,
urged and squeezed, crack apart.
Dazzling Lucifer's gut everts,
injects. It feeds. And sated, after,
that arrogant shuriken welds
fast to an ironshore boulder.

Jellyfish

shall inherit
the irradiated sea

placenta pumped
with clear ichor

eternal as
everclear plastics

pulsing scriptless
glow bubbles

after the final
solution of food

fish and deep-
sea squid

bagpipes of plasma
silently skreel

mute polyps
bloat and throb

sounding
the unrelenting

advance

Deluge

Clinging to cedars,
divans, bolsters,

whatever might float.
Barred from the ark,

each was chosen
to drown alone
in storm,

accepting the almost
all-consuming sea
as legacy.

Only the daughters
and sons of Noah
will inherit the Earth

and alight
on fiery Ararat

to repeat the offence.

Notes

"Red Dorking" is a heritage breed of chicken.

"Charlotte Small" was the wife of explorer and mapmaker David Thompson.

"Torrington": John Torrington, a member of Franklin's ill-fated Third Arctic Expedition of 1845-6, was the first to die in that mass disaster. In 1984, a team of scientists exhumed the stoker's frozen corpse. The autopsy revealed a body poisoned by lead and ravaged by emphysema, pneumonia, and TB.

"Glass Sponges": Ancient reefs of glass sponges found in Hecate Strait east of Haida Gwaii are being ravaged by the gear of deep sea trawlers.

Acknowledgements

I wish to thank the editors of the following journals in which earlier versions of many of these poems appeared:

"Sloth," *The Walrus* (online) (shortlisted for the 2015 Walrus Poetry Prize)

"Torrington," "Northern Shrike," "Red Pileated Woodpecker," and "Seahorse," *Agenda*

"Sea Star and Mussel," "Glacier Lily," "Great Auk," and "Garbage Bear," *Eunoia Review*

"Foxy," *Poetry Quarterly*

"Goldfinch," *Lantern Magazine*

"Paul on the Adriatic," *America Magazine* (winner of the 2014 Foley Poetry Prize)

"Franz Marc's *Wild Pigs (Boar and Sow), 1913*," *Poetry Salzburg Review*

"Giant Pandas," "Chilcotin Wild Horses," *Canary*

"Cain," *Poetica Magazine*

"Ship in a Bottle," *Vallum*

"Layer," *This Magazine* (2012 Great Canadian Literary Hunt 3rd place poetry winner)

"Spirit Bear," *Cirque*

"Bison: Calving," *Prairie Fire*

"The Ear of Malchus," *Wascana Review*

"Wooly Bear Caterpillar," "*Pommes de Terre*," and "Dandelions," *The New Quarterly*

"Bison: Wallowing," *Other Poetry*

"David," *Orbis*

"Omens of Cortés," *Grain Magazine*

"Charlotte Small," *The Prairie Journal*

"Tent Caterpillars," *The South Carolina Review*

"Horsefly" and "Wasps," *Poetry Nottingham*

"Maasai," *Arc Poetry Magazine*

"Foundations of Cages," *The Antigonish Review*

"La Brea Woman" and "Footprints at Laetoli, Tanzania," *Quarry*

"Hail," *Green's Magazine*

"A Damp Angelic Spring" and "Temptation," *Taproot*

My deep thanks to my editor Nick Thran for his sharp eye and attuned ear, and to all the fine folk at Brick Books. I am grateful to Don McKay for spurring me on and to the poets in the sessions led by Don at the Frith. Many of the poems in this collection have benefited greatly from the insights provided by poets Barbara Myers, Alison Goodman, Beverly Couse, and Amber Homeniuk. I also thank Zsuzsi Gartner for championing inventive points of view and Jack Hodgins who, in my high school days, showed the virtue of patience.

It was my good fortune to grow up in a boisterous, outdoorsy family with many brothers and sisters, all of whom live fully in the worlds of nature and art. To my parents, Isabelle and Ron, and my six siblings, Carol, Elizabeth, Hugh, Melanie, Bruce, and Juliet—thank you. To my own children, Beni, Tobi, and MC, and my wife Bernadette, I am so very grateful. Your regard for the planet, the spirit, and the muses is reflected in these poems.

Raised on Vancouver Island, DAN MacISAAC was educated at the University of Victoria and the University of Alberta. He has worked as a prospector and as a teacher. For over twenty-five years, he has been a trial lawyer in Victoria. His poetry, verse translations, and stories have appeared in a wide variety of literary magazines in Canada, the US, and the UK.